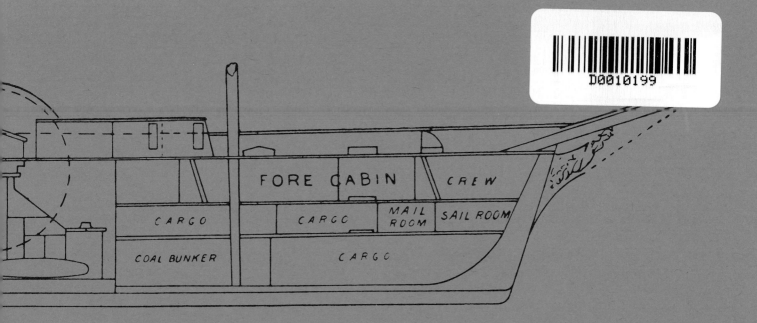

FORE CABIN   CREW

CARGO   CARGO   MAIL ROOM   SAIL ROOM

COAL BUNKER   CARGO

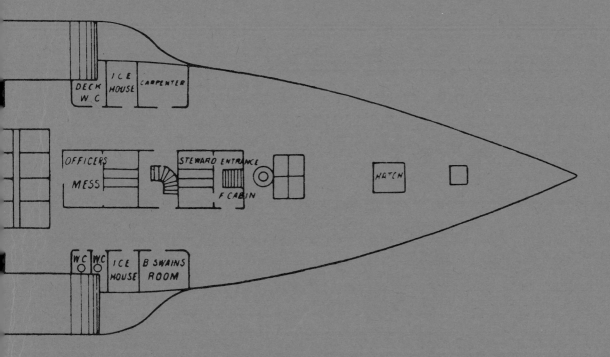

DECK W.C   ICE HOUSE   CARPENTER

OFFICERS MESS   STEWARD ENTRANCE   HATCH
F CABIN

WC WC   ICE HOUSE   B SWAINS ROOM

(front cover) *Northern Star* 1962 Shaw,
Savill & Albion Co. 24733 tons. Built
for her owners' round–the–world–
passengers-only service in which she
worked opposite the 20204-ton
Southern Cross of 1955. Photo: Shaw,
Savill & Albion Co.

(back cover) The iron hulled Cunard
mail paddle steam ship Persia of 1856
which easily outpaced her American
rivals of the Collins Line.

(front endpaper) *Britannia* 1840
Cunard Line. The pioneer Cunard
mail steamer; a 1135-ton wooden
hulled vessel with berths for 115 first
class passengers.

(back endpaper top) *Andes* 1939 Royal
Mail Lines. Built for the Southampton
to the River Plate trade, but rebuilt as
a cruise liner in 1959.

(back endpaper below) The iron screw
steamship *Orient* of 1879, the first built
for the Australian trade of the London
based Orient Steam Navigation
Company.

© Crown copyright 1980
First published 1980
ISBN 0 11 290316 9
Design by HMSO Graphic Design

Printed in England for
Her Majesty's Stationery Office
by W. S. Cowell Ltd, Ipswich

Dd 596287   K160

National Maritime Museum

THE SHIP

Channel Packets and Ocean Liners

1850-1970

John M. Maber

London
Her Majesty's Stationery Office

Contents

Introduction by the General Editor 3

The ocean paddler 5

Auxiliary screw to full powered steamship 13

The express liners 23

Between the Wars 39

Post War and decline 49

The passenger liner: epilogue 56

Index 59

The Orient Line steamship *Austral* (5524 tons) built for the Australian trade in 1881.

Introduction by the General Editor

This is the sixth of a series of ten short books on the development of the ship, both the merchant vessel and the specialised vessel of war, from the earliest times to the present day, commissioned and produced jointly by the National Maritime Museum and Her Majesty's Stationery Office.

The books are each self-contained, each dealing with one aspect of the subject, but together they cover the evolution of vessels in terms which are detailed, accurate and up-to-date. They incorporate the latest available information and the latest thinking on the subject, but they are readily intelligible to the non-specialist, professional historian or layman.

Above all, as should be expected from the only large and comprehensive general historical Museum in the world which deals especially with the impact of the sea on the development of human culture and civilisation, the approach is unromantic and realistic. Merchant ships were and are machines for carrying cargo profitably. They carried the trade and, in the words of the very distinguished author of the second book of the series, 'the creation of wealth through trade is the root of political and military power'. The vessel of war, the maritime vehicle of that power, follows, and she is a machine for men to fight from or with.

It follows from such an approach that the illustrations to this series are for the most part from contemporary sources. The reader can form his own conclusions from the evidence, written and visual. We have not commissioned hypothetical reconstructions, the annotation of which, done properly, would take up much of the text.

In this book, Commander Maber deals with the worldwide development and eventual decline of the passenger steamship. As with all the authors in this series, his approach, although in this case the centre of the scene is necessarily Britain, is international, for shipping and shipbuilding are international businesses in which developments in one country rapidly spread all over the world, as is very apparent from Commander Maber's account of the passenger carrying business.

Commander Maber's approach is in sharp contrast with that of Mr Craig in the fifth volume in this series. Commander Maber tells his story through the history of the individual ships themselves and through the changes which took place from one individual ship to another he presents the changing pattern of passenger carrying. Not only is his approach different from that of Mr Craig, even in places he differs in the interpretation he puts upon the history—for instances there is a difference of view over the success of the auxiliary steamship in long range trade.

Commander Maber is a distinguished authority on his subject, best known perhaps for his extremely detailed work on the passenger routes between Europe and Australasia, published as 'North Star to Southern Cross'.

Basil Greenhill
DIRECTOR, NATIONAL MARITIME MUSEUM
General Editor

The 3300 ton iron paddle steamer
Persia which entered Cunard service
between Liverpool and New York in
January 1856. The high standard of her
accommodation for 200 first and 50
second class passengers attracted much
favourable comment at the time.

The ocean paddler

The first primitive passenger steamship appeared on the rivers and estuaries of the United States in the first decade of the 19th century. By 1825 regular services were being worked not only on the great waterways and lakes of North America but also throughout much of western Europe. These services pre-dated the railways and did much to supplement, and indeed in many cases to supplant, travel by stage or canal. Regular sailings were advertised between Glasgow and Liverpool and from the latter port to the Isle of Man, Belfast, Dublin and Whitehaven; from Leith to Aberdeen and the northern Scottish ports and between Leith and London for which trade two steam vessels, each with sleeping accommodation for 100 passengers, were completed in May 1821. Further afield, in 1826 the General Steam Navigation Co, the first of the great chartered steamship companies, was advertising sailings between London, Lisbon and Gibraltar employing the paddle steamers *George IV* and *Duke of York*.

In fact, international sailings along the western European seaboard were but a beginning. Thus in 1829 the East India Company established a connection between Bombay and Suez employing the 411-ton Bombay-built paddle-steamer *Hugh Lindsay* which, although completely unsuited to the task, contrived to make at least one round voyage per year until 1836. Thereafter the service was taken over by the *Atalanta* and *Berenice*, larger and more powerful vessels designed for the trade, which proved themselves capable of maintaining an adequate two-monthly service. The complementary connection between Southampton and Alexandria was worked from September 1840 by the Peninsular & Oriental Steam Navigation Co, monthly departures alternating with those to Constantinople.

From these small beginnings the great international passenger network was to develop, and by 1850 regular services were being worked across the North Atlantic, to the West Indies and via Alexandria and Suez to India[1], Penang, Singapore and Hong Kong. There was of course no Suez Canal and the Egyptian authorities were responsible for the overland link between Alexandria and Suez. One and all, however, these services were made possible only by the award of substantial mail contracts on the part of the British and United States governments. The vessels themselves were wooden hulled paddle-steamers engined with simple side lever machinery of the type then fitted in the majority of merchant steamships and closely similar to the machinery of the paddle tug *Reliant* which can be seen today working in the National Maritime Museum. In addition all were given a full outfit of sails, usually a three-masted barque or barquentine rig, not only that advantage might be taken of favourable winds during the long ocean passages but also to enable way to be maintained whilst blowing down the salt water fed boilers and during the all too frequent mechanical breakdowns.

[1] To Madras and Calcutta. The Suez to Bombay route continued to be worked by the East India Co until 1852 when the company's mail contract was terminated.

The mail contracts awarded by the British Admiralty[2] laid down that the steamers were to be capable of being armed for naval service in the event of war and to some extent of course this requirement dictated their design parameters. In particular the vessels were to be built of wood with sufficient strength to '. . . carry guns of the largest calibre' and were to be designed for rapid conversion to a naval role. Typical of this class was the Royal Mail Steam Packet Co's *Thames*, a 1889-ton paddler completed by Wm. Pitcher at Northfleet which first cleared Gravesend for Georgetown, Guiana, with mail and passengers in December 1841. Engined with twin-cylinder simple side lever machinery she could maintain a service speed of some $8\frac{1}{2}$ knots under steam alone and was classed as a 'full powered steamship', i.e. she did not have to rely on sail to maintain her schedule. Accommodation was provided for 92 passengers. The *Thames* worked between Southampton and the West Indies and on the Caribbean inter-island services until the outbreak of the Crimean War in 1854 when she was taken up for transport work.

[2] The Admiralty was responsible for the carriage of the overseas mails from 1823 until 1860 when control was returned to the Post Office.

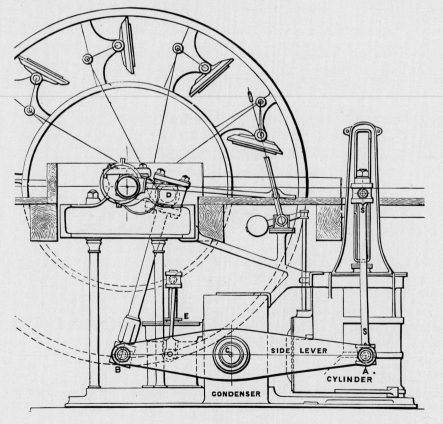

Side lever engine and paddle wheel ('The Marine Steam Engine', 1898). Machinery of this type was widely fitted in ocean paddle-steamers built in United Kingdom shipyards throughout the 1840s.

Thereafter, the now ageing vessel returned to the mail service although, together with her sister ship the 1744-ton *Teviot*, she did make a brief appearance on the Southampton to Alexandria route on behalf of the European & Australian Royal Mail Co. in January 1859. The *Thames* was finally sold for breaking up locally in the West Indies in 1865.

For some reason the provision that mail packets be built of wood did not apply in the case of the Peninsular & Oriental S. N. Co. which was awarded a contract in 1840 for the Southampton to Malta and Alexandria mail service. In so far as other operators were concerned, however, the requirement was backed up between 1842 and 1850 by a series of trials which demonstrated that the impact of shot and shell on the wrought iron plate then available resulted in jagged holes with considerable splintering and some-

times the tearing of the plating from the ship's frames, making the control of flooding difficult if not impossible. In the event, the destruction by fire of the 2256-ton wooden hulled *Amazon* on the 4 January 1852 at the outset of her maiden voyage in the Royal Mail S. P. Co's. West Indies service brought about a change of policy and the acceptance of iron hulls . for mail packets.

For a few years more the primary services across the Atlantic and to the Mediterranean continued to be worked by paddle-steamers, long favoured by the Admiralty for their manoeuvrability although they tended to lose speed in a seaway due to broken water choking the paddle boxes.

Dee 1841 Royal Mail Steam Packet Co. One of the fleet of 14 similar paddle-steamers built between 1841 and 1843 for the company's West Indies trade. Photo: NMM

Contemporary coastal and cross-channel packets differed little from the ocean mail steamers apart from size and rig, the archetype of the 1850s being a schooner-rigged paddler, usually iron-hulled since there was no contractual requirement for naval service in the event of a national emergency. Size and speed were determined by the intended route, vessels built for day passage being in general faster than those designed for the longer overnight crossings. Of the faster vessels in service in 1850, the 320-tons gross *Dispatch* was one of three 13-knot quasi-sisters built in 1847 by Messrs Ditchburn & Mare of Blackwall for the Southampton to Havre/Channel Island trades of the New South Western Packet Co. She served her owners, from 1862 the London & South Western Railway Co., with apparent satisfaction until 1885.

In 1842 the Peninsular & Oriental S. N. Co. had been awarded a further mail contract for an eastern extension from Suez to Madras and Calcutta, worked initially by wooden paddle-steamers such as the 2017-ton *Hindostan*, a twin-cylinder direct-acting engined vessel built in 1842 by Thos. Wilson of Liverpool for service on the Indian station. However, iron replaced wood in the mid-1840s by which time the mail service had been extended via Penang and Singapore to Hong Kong, connecting with the Calcutta steamer from Suez at Point de Galle in Ceylon. Shanghai was reached in 1850. The first vessel of this new fleet of

Hindostan 1842 Peninsular & Oriental S.N.Co. The 2018-ton paddle-steamer *Hindostan* and her sister, the *Bentinck*, opened the company's Suez to Calcutta service.
Photo: NMM

iron-hulled paddle-steamers designed for service in eastern waters was the 797-ton *Erin*, a side lever engined craft completed in 1846 and employed in the Bombay to Hong Kong route. In 1850 the Peninsular & Oriental eastern fleet comprised five wooden and seven iron-hulled paddlers working a network of services with its focal point at Point de Galle. In view of the lack of repair facilities for iron hulls east of Suez, however, the wooden steamers did in the event serve longer in those waters than elsewhere and, in fact, the wooden hulled *Braganza* (1836/855 tons), *Achilles* (1838/992 tons) and *Oriental* (1840/1787 tons) were transferred east of Suez following their replacement by faster iron-hulled paddle-steamers on the Southampton to Alexandria stage.

Founded in 1840 as the British & North American Royal Mail Steam Packet Co., the Cunard Line was the most successful of the early North Atlantic Mail Companies to the extent that at the beginning of 1850 the western ocean was virtually a Cunard preserve.

Other companies put in an ephemeral appearance but not until the advent of the American Collins Line in April 1850 was any real challenge mounted in the face of Cunard supremacy. The 2845-ton *Atlantic*, a wooden hulled side lever engined paddle-steamer with accommodation for 200 first class passengers, took the company's first sailing from New York on the 27 April 1850. In the matter of luxury, the passenger accommodation was far superior to that provided in contemporary Cunard vessels, the cabins and public rooms being steam-heated whilst other refinements included bathrooms, a smoking room and ladies' rooms, and a barber's shop. A few months later, in September 1850, the 2707-ton *Pacific*, sister of the *Atlantic*, took the westbound record with a crossing

Canada 1848 Cunard Line. The 1831-ton wooden hulled *Canada* which established a record in July 1849 by crossing from Halifax to Liverpool at an average speed of 12.41 knots. Photo: *Illustrated London News*

between Liverpool and New York of 10 days 4 hours 45 minutes. Cunard replied to the American challenge by building the 2226-ton wooden paddlers *Asia* and *Africa*, which were followed two years later from the same Greenock shipyard of Robert Steele & Son by the 2402-ton *Arabia*, the last wooden hulled vessel built for the Cunard fleet. Fitted with powerful twin side lever engines, the cylinders being no less than 8 ft 7 ins diameter and taking steam at 18 psi from the four iron tubular box boilers, there was in fact little to choose between the *Arabia* and her Collins' rivals in the matter of passage times.

At this time the paddle-steamer still retained an advantage in the matter of speed and in January 1856 Robert Napier & Sons of Glasgow delivered the 3300-ton iron-hulled *Persia* built with the express intention of bringing the Atlantic record back to Cunard. This she achieved in the following July with a westbound crossing to New York of 9 days 1 hour 45 minutes at an average speed of 13.82 knots. Once again the machinery was of the twin-cylinder simple side lever type with cylinders, 8 ft 4½ ins diameter by 10 ft stroke, taking steam at 20 psi from eight tubular box boilers. By this time the Admiralty had abandoned its objections to the use of iron for the hulls of mail steamers and one by one the ageing wooden paddlers, their timber frames wracked by the motion of powerful machinery, were sold for breaking up or

Baltic 1850 Collins Line. One of the group of four paddle-steamers with which Collins challenged Cunard supremacy on the North Atlantic. Photo: NMM

were turned over to employment on less exacting duties.

In the United States, however, iron was expensive whereas ample supplies of suitable timber were readily available. Thus in 1865 when the U.S. Post-master General accepted a bid, in fact the only one, submitted by the Pacific Mail Steamship Co. for a monthly service between San Francisco and Hong Kong, the contract called for the construction of four wooden paddle-steamers of perhaps remarkable design. Unlike contemporary British ocean-going steamers with their clipper stems and basic sailing ship characteristics, the American vessels were en-larged versions of the well-proven sound and river side wheelers of the coastal states. Fitted with single-cylinder vertical walking beam machinery built by the Novelty Iron Works of New York, these early Pacific Mail steamers were distinctive by virtue of the fact that the massive rocking beam was sited on deck between the paddle boxes. They were the largest

Duchess of York 1895 South Eastern Rly. Co. The 996-ton paddle-steamer *Duchess of York* built by R.&H.Green of Blackwall for her owners' Folkestone to Boulogne service. Photo: NPA

wooden merchant steamers ever built and with their straight stems and light barque rig were essentially American, not only in concept and appearance but also in the spacious comfort of their accommodation. First to enter service was the 3881-ton *Great Republic*, built by Henry Steers of Greenpoint, Long Island, which left New York for San Francisco on the 18 May 1867 prior to taking her departure from the latter port for Yokohama and Hong Kong.

Of the Pacific Mail quartette, the *America* (4454 tons) and *Japan* (4351 tons) were destroyed by fire in 1872 and 1874, respectively, whilst the *Great Republic* was withdrawn from service in 1876 only to be wrecked under another houseflag in April 1879. The sole survivor, the 3836-ton *China*, was withdrawn from service in 1879, eventually to be sold for breaking up in 1886, thus putting a period to the era of the ocean-going wooden paddle-steamers.

Cunard built its last paddle-steamer, the magnificent 3871-ton iron-hulled *Scotia*, in 1862 when such craft were still the fastest afloat. A beautiful clipper-stemmed brig-rigged vessel with accommodation for 573 first class passengers, she was capable of a service speed of 14 knots and ensured continued Cunard dominance on the North Atlantic ferry. Popular as she was with the travelling public, however, the *Scotia* with her massive side lever machinery was already outmoded before she entered service. The Peninsular & Oriental Steam Nav. Co. and the Royal Mail Steam Packet Co. too, built their last ocean paddle-steamers in the 1860s, although by this time the screw steamer had all but ousted the paddler in so far as the important ocean mail services were concerned. Thus in March 1862, two months before the completion of the *Scotia* by the same builders, Cunard took delivery from Robert Napier & Sons of the 2638-ton barque-rigged *China*, the first purpose-designed screw steamer for the company's North Atlantic mail and passenger trade.

Only in the cross-channel and coastal passenger trades did the paddle-steamer continue to flourish. Speed and manoeuvrability in restricted waters were its essential attributes and it was these factors that ensured its popularity for many years to come. In fact not until after the turn of the century was the express paddle-steamer finally displaced on the English Channel short sea connections from Dover, and even then it was only the advent of the direct drive turbine steamer that led to its eventual demise. The last important paddle-steamers built for this trade were *Le Nord* and *Le Pas de Calais*, completed for the French Chemin de Fer du Nord by the Ateliers et Chantiers de la Loire in 1898 Each of 2004 gross tons and engined with triple expansion diagonal machinery, they were capable of a service of 21 knots. These details apart, the sisters were unique in that they were the only cross-channel paddlers ever built in in France! Both were withdrawn from service in 1923.

Paddle-steamers continued to be built for another half century, but only for relatively sheltered water ferry duties and coastal excursion work for which their manoeuvrability alongside piers in restricted shallow waters was an essential factor. The more economical screw steamship had driven the paddle-steamer from the ocean trades and in due course it was the diesel-engined ferry/excursion craft which displaced the paddler in these coastal trades.

As an ocean-going vessel the paddle-steamer had played a major part in establishing the international network of mail and passenger services, but this had been achieved only with the aid of relatively generous subsidies awarded in the guise of mail contracts. By 1880 the ocean paddler had all but disappeared, but for many years more such craft worked the short sea and coastal passenger services until eventually economic pressures forced these vessels too into retirement and thence to the shipbreaker's yard.

Auxiliary screw to full powered steamship

In the early years of the 19th century a number of patents were taken out proposing the use of various forms of screw propeller. Obviously many of these were impractical but others contributed to the eventual success of the screw steamship. In England the most important patent was that taken out by Francis Pettit Smith on the 31 May 1836 for a '. . . sort of screw or worm made to revolve rapidly under water, in a recess or open space formed in that part of the after-part of the vessel, commonly called the dead rising, or dead wood . . .'. In the wake of successful trials with the launch *Francis Smith* on the Paddington Canal, the Ship Propeller Co. was formed in 1838 to build a larger seagoing vessel.

The 240-ton *Archimedes*, built on the Thames in 1839, was fitted with a twin-cylinder simple expansion engine with a crankshaft speed of 26 rpm. This was, however, too low for efficient working of the screw and gearing was required to give the shaft speed of 140 rpm. The Admiralty took considerable interest in the trials of the *Archimedes*, but following demonstrations at Portsmouth and Plymouth she visited Bristol where Brunel's iron-hulled steamship *Great Britain*, then known as the *Mammoth*, was under construction. A further series of trials was sufficient to convince Brunel that the screw propeller should be adopted for the *Great Britain*.

The *Great Britain* was floated out from her building dock into the Bristol Floating Harbour in July 1843, although it was the 26 July 1845 before she took her maiden sailing from Liverpool bound for New York.

Of 3270 tons she was in fact the first iron-hulled screw steamer built for the ocean trades and with accommodation for 360 first class passengers was the pioneer ocean screw liner. At the outset of her fifth westbound crossing, however, the *Great Britain* stranded in Dundrum Bay on the County Down coast and for the time being disappeared from the Atlantic scene.

Brief though her Atlantic career may have been, the *Great Britain* had achieved some success, and in 1850 the Glasgow shipbuilders Tod & McGregor completed for their own account the 1609-ton barque-rigged iron screw steamship *City of Glasgow* which, on the 15 April in that year, was despatched from Glasgow for New York. The vessel was unsubsidised and accommodation was provided for 52 first and 85 second class passengers, in addition to which 400 steerage passengers could be berthed in temporary accommodation in the cargo 'tween deck spaces, although no use appears to have been made of this facility whilst she remained under her builders' houseflag. In December 1850, however, the *City of Glasgow* passed into the ownership of the Liverpool & Philadelphia Steam Ship Co. (Inman Line) which decided in 1852 to make a bid for a share of the emigrant trade, then the exclusive preserve of the established sailing ship companies. Spurned by the mail steamers, not only across the North Atlantic but also the Australian and South American trades, the emigrants had no other choice until eventually vessels such as the *City of Glasgow* finally put a period to the steerage trade under sail.

Back in 1847, James Hodgson of Liverpool had delivered the 1299-ton *Sarah Sands*, the second large iron screw vessel built. Classed as an auxiliary screw steamship, the *Sarah Sands* had been laid down apparently for the Australian trade although in the event she was first employed on the North Atlantic. Such craft were designed to travel under sail as much as possible using steam only when winds were light or adverse, thus permitting a reasonably tight schedule without the need for stowage of vast quantities of coal. The auxiliary screw steamer achieved some limited success in the North Atlantic trade but it was on the long haul to Australia via the Cape that such vessels proved most popular both with emigrants increasingly attracted to Australia by the discovery of gold in 1851, and with first class

passengers, many of whom preferred the leisurely comfort of Money Wigram's auxiliaries to the formal luxury of the Peninsular & Oriental steamers. Of the many steam clippers employed in the Australian trade at one time or another from 1852 onwards those of Money Wigram's fleet proved by far the most successful. Passages to Melbourne by the 2342-ton *Somersetshire*, which entered service in July 1867, averaged 45 to 50 days compared with some 80 days under sail and 52[3] days via the mail service. The latter involved the overland crossing from Alexandria to Suez and a change of steamer at Point de Galle in

[3] This might be reduced to 48 days by travelling overland to Marseilles whence a connecting service was worked to Alexandria.

Ceylon. In fact, not until the 1880s did the Peninsular & Oriental provide a regular direct service to Australian ports!

In the meantime, in 1852, the African Steam Ship Co.[4] had obtained a contract, valued at £21,259 per annum, for the carriage of the West African mails, and in September of that year the 400-ton iron screw steamer *Forerunner* took her first sailing from London to Accra and Fernando Po. She was followed by the *Faith, Hope* and *Charity*, all built, like the *Forerunner*, by John Laird of Birkenhead and providing accommodation for a limited number of first class passengers. McGregor Laird, brother of John Laird and the driving force behind the African Steam Ship Co., was a deeply religious man and presumably it was his belief in the development of the West African trade as a potential factor in the eradication of the slave trade which led to the choice of names for the new company's steamships. In the event, the formation of the African Steam Ship Co. was closely followed by the outbreak of the Crimean War, and *Faith, Hope* and *Charity*, despite their names, were diverted to transport work along with many of the steamships then operating under the British flag.

The pioneer in the steam trade to South Africa was the General Screw Steam Shipping Co. which had successfully tendered in 1850 for the Cape mail contract, the first sailing being taken by the small 445-ton iron auxiliary screw steamship *Bosphorus* despatched from London in December of that year. In February 1852 the company secured an extension of its contract from the Cape to Ceylon and Calcutta, and in the following September it was reported that there were under construction '. . . two vessels of large size (2500 tons) for the Australian trade[5].' These two craft, completed in 1854 as *Golden Fleece* and *The Prince*, each provided well-appointed accommodation for 200 passengers, although they were never to see service on the route for which they had been designed. Like many of their contemporaries they were taken up on government charter for transport work but following their release they were sold for trading under another flag.

Other vessels of the General Screw company did work briefly in the Australian trade, the last sailing being taken by the 1815-ton iron auxiliary *Argo* which departed Southampton for Port Philip and Sydney on October 1854. An advertisement concerning this craft featured in *The Times* on the 27

[4] Advertised as the Iron Steam Ship Company's African Line. (*The Times*, 20 April 1852)
[5] *The Times*, 21 September 1852.

(left) *Great Britain* 1845 Great Western Steam Ship Co. Brunel's iron screw steamship which was floated out of her building dock in Bristol on the 19 July 1843. Photo: NMM

(right) *City of Glasgow* 1850 Tod & McGregor. Built for her builder's own account, the 1609-ton *City of Glasgow* became the first vessel of the Liverpool-based Inman Line. Photo: NMM

April 1853 and is worth quoting in full for its description of the auxiliary screw steamer concept:

'General Screw Steam Shipping Company Announcement. Such a fatality has latterly attended the various steamships bound to Australia causing an amount of loss and inconvenience to the mercantile public that the Directors of the General Screw Company determined to test *fully* the qualities of the "Argo" before sending her to sea. She left the Nore on Friday, proceeded down channel under steam alone, with the wind moderate ahead, at 10 knots. Under all plain sail, with a fresh wind and the screw feathered, she maintained 11 knots. The time to feather the screw was 7 minutes from the stopping of the engines. There is also means to raise the screw out of the water for inspection at sea. There were no overheated bearings or want of steam during the trial. The passage from Southampton to Port Philip is expected to be completed in fifty-five to sixty-five days.'

Steam services under the British flag were largely disrupted by the demands of the Crimean War, but in the wake of the 1856 Congress of Paris the long-established chartered companies sought new mail contracts, although in the case of the Australian service the Peninsular & Oriental S. N. Co. suffered a setback when the award went to a new and inexperienced concern, the European & Australian Royal Mail Co. Completely unprepared for the acceptance of its tender the new company was forced to charter from the P&O, Cunard and the Royal Mail S. P. Co. pending the completion of vessels for its own account then under construction on the Clyde. Typical of these steamships was the 2902-ton iron screw steamer *Australasian*, a ship-rigged full-powered vessel en-

(left) *Nemesis* 1857 Peninsular & Oriental S.N.Co. The iron screw steamship *Nemesis* built by Wm.Denny photographed at Dumbarton after being traded in to her builders in part payment for new tonnage. Photo: NMM

(right) *Khersonese* 1857 North Atlantic S.N.Co. The 1409-ton auxiliary screw steamship *Khersonese* built for the short-lived Liverpool, Newfoundland & Halifax S.N.Co. Photo: NMM

gined with simple twin-cylinder inverted machinery, which was completed by J. & G. Thomson in 1857. At the time the *Australasian* and her sister, the 2956-ton *Tasmanian*, were the most powerful screw steamers afloat and under steam alone were able to maintain a steady 11 knots in fair weather. Accommodation was provided for 200 first and sixty second class passengers. In the event, the company's resources proved inadequate and in September 1857 management of its affairs was taken over by the Royal Mail S. P. Co. Eventually, tenders for a new Australian contract were invited and this time proposals for a monthly service submitted by the Peninsular & Oriental were accepted in return for an annual subvention of £180000. The first sailing from Southamp-

ton (for Alexandria) was taken on the 12 March 1859 by the 2014-ton iron screw steamer *Pera*, the 1491-ton *Salsette* having departed on the 12 February to open the homeward service east of Suez.

Throughout this period of change the Peninsular & Oriental adhered strictly to its policy of not catering for third class passengers and indeed this was still the accepted rule in April 1880 when the following notice appeared in the London press:

'The Peninsular & Oriental Company steamers under contract for the Australian Mail Service do not carry Third Class or Steerage passengers.'

Other companies such as the Orient Steam Navigation Co., which entered the Australian trade via the Cape in June 1877 employing full powered steam-

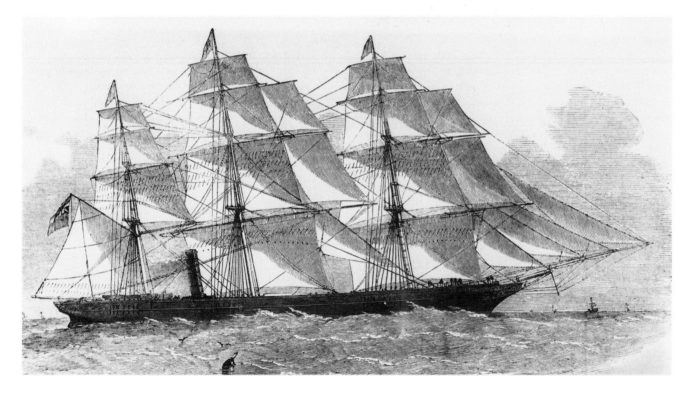

ships surplus to the requirements of the Pacific Steam Navigation Co., exploited the emigrant trade to best advantage and thereby generated a profit without the benefit for several years of any mail subsidy.

Mention has been made (p. 15) of the pioneer auxiliary screw steamship services to the Cape and beyond. In the event, few of the companies involved survived the aftermath of the Crimean War and in its wake, the Indian Mutiny, which had given rise to further demands on the part of the government. Back in October 1853, however, a new company to be known as the Union Steam Collier Co. had been formed in Southampton to bring coal from South Wales to meet the needs of the Peninsular & Oriental, the Royal Mail and other lines. Orders were placed for five iron-hulled steam colliers which saw little service in their intended trade before they were diverted elsewhere, eventually, with the exception of the 403-ton *Saxon*, to be taken up for the transport service. Once released, all ideas of carrying coal were abandoned and the steamers were turned over briefly to a Brazilian venture working out monthly from Southampton to Rio de Janeiro in opposition to the subsidised mail paddlers of the Royal Mail S. P. Co. In 1857, however, the Admiralty invited tenders for a monthly steam service to the Cape and the Union company, now reorganised in the wake of the Joint Stock Companies Act of 1856 as the Union Steam Ship Co. Ltd., submitted an offer to work the route in return for an annual subvention of £30 000. This bid was accepted and the first sailing from Southampton on the 15 September 1857 was taken by the 530-ton *Dane* carrying albeit, only six passengers in addition to the mails!

The Union Line prospered and by the mid-1860s the service was being worked by full-powered iron screw steamships such as the 1282-ton *Roman*, a brig-rigged vessel providing accommodation for 60 first and 40 second class passengers. As in the case of the Peninsular & Oriental mail steamers no provision was made for steerage passengers. The first class quarters were occupied mainly by government officials and their families, army officers or others with business interests abroad, whilst the second class catered primarily for the staff and personal servants of the first class passengers. In passing, it should be noted that few North Atlantic steamers of this mid-Victorian period offered this type of second class accommodation.

At this time, in the mid-1860s, the Royal Mail Steam Packet Co. based on Southampton was working out fortnightly to St. Thomas in the West Indies and monthly to Rio de Janeiro employing a fleet still largely paddle-propelled. Not until 1865 did the company take delivery of the first iron screw steamers built for its own account, the vessels concerned being the brig-rigged *Douro* (2824 tons) and *Rhone* (2738 tons). Engined with twin-cylinder simple inverted direct-acting machinery driving single screws, the sisters were good for a service speed of 12 knots, given reasonable weather, under steam alone. Accommodation was provided for 253 first, 30 second and 30 steerage passengers, the latter intended presumably for Portuguese emigrants seeking passage from Lisbon to Rio de Janeiro.

In 1886 the West Indies service itinerary was extended through to Colon, the Atlantic terminal of the Panama Railroad, thus permitting a direct connection with the west coast steamers of the Pacific Steam Navigation Co. which worked between Panama, Guayaquil, Callao and Valparaiso.

With the opening, also in 1866, of the Panama, New Zealand & Australia Royal Mail Co's. service across the Pacific to Wellington and Sydney, including an intermediate coaling stop at Rapa some 700 miles to the south-south-east of Tahiti, the British flag network was practically complete. In an attempt to secure maximum fuel economy for the long stages across the Pacific the company's steamers *Rakaia*,

Mataura and *Ruahine* were fitted with compound machinery, although stowage of coal was to remain a critical factor throughout the short history of the company. In passing, it is also worthy of note that the 1504-ton *Ruahine* was the first ocean-going twin screw vessel although why she should have been so designed when her consorts were all given single screws is not known.

British companies by no means had matters all their own way in mid-Victorian times, however, since both French and German operators had built up extensive service networks. The Cie des Services Maritimes des Messageries Impériales, later to become well known as the Cie des Messageries Maritimes, had grown from a localised Mediterranean business first through the award in 1857 of a mail contract for a service to the River Plate. Then in 1862

the signing of a further contract foreshadowed the introduction of a service to India, Indo-China and Hong Kong via the Egyptian overland route between Alexandria and Suez. This eastern sevice opened in October 1862 with the departure from Marseilles of the 1085-ton iron screw steamship *Neva*, the connection east of Suez worked by the 2188-ton *Impératrice*.

Unlike the Messageries Maritimes, the Hamburg-Amerika Linie (HAPAG) first achieved prominence on the North Atlantic where the emigrant trade represented an important sector of its activities. The first sailings were taken by the Clyde-built iron screw steamers *Borussia* (2131 tons) and *Hammonia* (2026

Hammonia 1867 Hamburg Amerika Linie. Like many of the early HAPAG ocean passenger steamships, the 3035-ton *Hammonia* was built on the Clyde by Caird of Greenock. Photo: NMM

tons) which departed Hamburg on the 1 June and 1 July 1856 respectively. Each provided accommodation for 54 first, 146 second class and 310 steerage passengers.

Two years later, on the 19 June 1858, the rival Bremen-based Norddeutscher Lloyd despatched the 2674-ton *Bremen* to inaugurate their own New York service. Like Hamburg-Amerika, the Norddeutscher Lloyd did not spurn the emigrant trade and the *Bremen* provided for 160 first and 110 second class passengers together with no fewer than 400 steerage berths. Services to the West Indies and the River Plate were introduced in the 1870s and in the next decade the company turned its attention eastwards to the Far East and Australasia.

The working of the overland passage between Alexandria and Suez had been greatly facilitated by the completion in December 1858 of the railway across the isthmus. In the following year, however, work began on an even greater project which was to eliminate the tedious transhipment of passengers, mails and goods. This was the Suez Canal, completed ten years later and formally opened in November 1869. This event made way for the introduction of through express services on these routes.

The passenger steamship throughout the third quarter of the 19th century could offer little by way of creature comforts. First and second class public rooms were usually ornate and relatively spacious, but the cabin accommodation was invariably cramped and ill-ventilated. Oil lamps or candles provided the sole means of illumination once the sun had set, but even these were extinguished at an early hour as a precaution against fire. Food there was in plenty in so

(left) *Mongolia* 1865 Peninsular & Oriental S.N.Co. Built for the Italian-subsidised Venice to Alexandria branch service. Photo: NMM

(right) *Péreire* 1866 Cie. Générale Transatlantique. Built on the Clyde and named after the brothers Emile and Isaac Péreire who founded the company's prosperity. Photo: NMM

far as the first and second class passengers were concerned, although in the absence of any form of refrigeration much of it was necessarily preserved, or highly spiced. Liquor, too, was freely available for these privileged travellers, and indeed some companies provided such liquid refreshment free of extra charge, possibly to restrict the use of the limited supply of potable water! This practice, inherited from the days of sail, had been abandoned by the North Atlantic companies in the 1840s, but it persisted in so far as the Peninsular & Oriental was concerned until 1871.

Steerage passengers were expected, however, to provide their own bedding and creature comforts although, certainly for European migrants, a basic cooked menu was made available which could be supplemented from the passengers' own resources or by purchase on board. After all, what more could one expect for a fare of six guineas in a better class steamer to New York or for about £20 to Sydney!

The era of the early screw steamer had been a time of expansion and consolidation. Other than the United States flag vessels employed across the Pacific, the majority of ocean passenger steamships at this time were simple engined craft of about two to three thousand registered tons, usually barque or brig-rigged, with a service speed under steam alone of 10 or 11 knots. The 1870s brought increased international competition on the ocean routes and it was this that provided the necessary stimulus for far-reaching improvements in design, comfort and the standard of service provided.

Lake Huron 1881 Beaver Line. Built for the Liverpool to Montreal (summer) service. Photo: NMM

The express liners

In December 1869 the 3081-ton Inman liner *City of Brussels* took the eastbound North Atlantic record from Cunard which had held the honour for the previous 13 years. At this time the weekly Cunard mail service between Liverpool and New York was being worked by the 2371-ton paddler *Scotia* of 1862, the 2638-ton screw steamer *China* completed also in 1862, the 2960-ton *Russia* of 1867 and such worthy but prosaic vessels as the *Cuba*, *Java* and *Samaria*, completed, respectively, in 1864, 1865 and 1868. Of this group only the outmoded *Scotia* had any valid claim as a record breaker, but the advent of the *City of Brussels* still came as a salutory reminder that prestige is ephemeral where the public whim is concerned. More was to come, however, for in March 1871 the White Star Line burst forth on the North Atlantic with the departure from Liverpool of the 3707-ton *Oceanic*, a 14-knot compound engined vessel built by Messrs. Harland & Wolff with a length-to-beam ratio of about 10 to 1, instead of the usual ratio of 8 to 1, in keeping with Belfast's principle of a 'long ship'. Whatever the supposed advantages, the 'long ship' was understandably subject to heavy vibration aft where custom decreed the first class passengers should be accommodated. In fact, this problem was overcome in the *Oceanic* by siting the first class saloon and the best cabins amidships instead of aft, thus breaking with a tradition inherited from the days of sail. Primarily, it was this development coupled with the economy of the compound engine which ensured the success of the White Star Line on the North Atlantic.

Early White Star voyages were marred by technical problems, but in May 1872 the 3888-ton *Adriatic* took the westbound record by crossing between Queenstown (Cobh) and New York in 7 days 23 hours 17 minutes. In the following January the 3707-ton *Baltic* followed up this achievement with a crossing from New York which cut nearly two hours off the record set by the City of Brussels in December 1869. Like all vessels intended for the White Star Line the Adriatic and Baltic were built at Belfast by Messrs. Harland & Wolff who were given complete freedom in the preparation of their design.

Thereafter, the White Star and the Inman maintained a mutual struggle for supremacy until July 1879 when the 5179-ton Guion liner *Arizona* wrested the eastbound record from the White Star *Britannic*. Three years later, the same company's 6932-ton *Alaska*, a 16-knot single screw steamer engined with three-cylinder compound machinery, captured the record in both directions.

In the meantime, there had been developments on the Eastern and Australasian routes where the established British lines vied with their French rivals for patronage. At the time of the completion of the Suez Canal in 1869 the Peninsular & Oriental and the Messageries Impériales (which became the Cie. des Messageries Maritimes in the wake of the downfall of the French monarchy in 1871) shared the bulk of the first class traffic seeking passage east of Suez from European ports. The canal had been no less than ten years under construction but few preparations had been made in anticipation of its completion and in particular the Peninsular & Oriental found itself with few vessels suitable for through working. A crisis concentrates the mind wonderfully, however, and the company embarked on a programme of new construction which resulted first in the delivery in 1870 of the 3664-ton *Australia*, an 11-knot craft fitted with twin-cylinder inverted compound machinery of the type adopted at this time as the standard propulsion unit for the P&O fleet. The *Australia* was the last of the company's barque-rigged clipper-stemmed steamers, her immediate successor being the straight-stemmed *Indus*, a 3471-ton iron-hulled vessel completed in 1871 and equipped with boilers working at the then high pressure of 65 psi. In keeping with the company's stated policy, accommodation was provided for some 150 first class and 50 second class passengers only.

In 1880 the Peninsular & Oriental took delivery for the through Bombay service of the sisters *Rohilla*, *Rosetta* and *Ravenna*, of which the latter (3372 tons) was the first steel-hulled vessel in the P&O fleet.

Engined with twin-cylinder compound machinery, they were good for a service speed of 13 knots and looked typical graceful steamers of their day. Sail was still carried but primarily to provide a little extra push when winds were favourable. Apart from the introduction of punkah louvre mechanical ventilation, however, accommodation standards were still somewhat austere and probably little better than that offered twenty years earlier. Certainly, the passage through the Red Sea must have been decidedly unpleasant.

In the event, contemporary passenger steamships of the Peninsular & Oriental S. N. Co. were completely outclassed by the Orient Steam Navigation Co's. 5524-ton *Austral*, a 16-knot steel-hulled vessel built on the Clyde in 1881 by John Elder & Co. The accommodation for 120 first class, 130 second class and 300 third class passengers was exceptionally spacious and well-ventilated for the time, although travellers were still forced to rely upon oil lighting in the cabins and public rooms. In this connection it is worthy of note that the White Star Line's record-breaking *Adriatic* and her sister *Celtic*, both completed for the North Atlantic trade in 1872, were equipped with coal-gas lighting but frequent pipe fractures resulting from the working of the vessel's hulls ensured its early removal.

The Cie des Messageries Maritimes entered the Australian trade in 1882, having been awarded a French government contract for a service to Australian ports and New Caledonia, the route being from Marseilles via Port Said to Mahé, Reunion, Mauritius, Adelaide, Melbourne, Sydney and Noumea. Seven 13-knot iron-hulled steamships of some 4100 tons

Bothnia 1874 Cunard Line. A compound engined single screw steamship typical of the sturdy but unimpressive vessels which worked the company's services throughout the 1870s. Photo: NMM

(above) *Britannic* 1874 White Star Line. The 5004-ton *Britannic* and her sister, the *Germanic*, were the most successful of the Harland & Wolff built "long ships". The *Germanic* remained afloat as the Turkish-owned *Gulcemal* until 1950. Photo: Author

(below) *Oceana* 1883 Peninsular & Oriental S.N.Co. One of the P&O 'Jubilee' quartette built for the Australian trade in 1887–88. Photo: NMM

apiece were ordered from the company's own shipyard at La Ciotat, near Marseilles, and were launched between 1881 and 1884 as the *Natal, Melbourne, Caledonien, Sydney, Salazie, Yarra* and *Oceanien,* collectively one of the largest groups of passenger vessels built to meet the requirements of a new service. The sisters were straight-stemmed barque-rigged vessels with twin funnels set close together and the heavy appearance typical of the company's 19th and early 20th century steamships. Each provided accommodation for some 90 first, 38 second and 75 third class passengers. Success attended the Messageries Maritimes enterprise and this first group of steamships was followed by a quartette of 6400-ton steel-hulled vessels, likewise built at La Ciotat and engined with triple expansion machinery for a service

speed of 16 knots. The *Australien, Polynesien, Ville de la Ciotat* and *Armand Behic,* which entered service between 1890 and 1892, each provided accommodation for 170 first, 70 second and 112 third class passengers with a degree of comfort equal to any available in vessels of the company's competitors.

The South African trade, too, benefited in the wake of competition both from lines trading to the Cape and from those serving Australia and New Zealand via Cape ports. The Union Steamship Co. had entered the trade in 1857 and by 1872 had become

Vicksburg 1872 Dominion Line. Built for the New Orleans trade but subsequently switched to the service between Liverpool and Canada which became known eventually as the Dominion Line. Photo: Author

Ballarat 1882 Peninsular & Oriental S.N.Co. A typical
P&O Australian steamship in the Suez Canal. Photo: NMM

well established as the operator of such well-found vessels as the 2039-ton *Danube*, a former Royal Mail paddler built in 1866 and converted to screw propulsion following her purchase without change of name by the Union Line in 1871. In March 1873, this vessel made the fastest Union passage to date, covering the 5970 miles between Southampton and Table Bay in $25\frac{1}{2}$ days. In the meantime, however, Donald Currie, a shipowner prominent in the East India trade, chartered from the Leith, Hull & Hamburg Steam Packet Co. (with which he was closely associated), the small screw steamships *Gothland* and *Iceland* in an attempt to restore the fortunes of the short-lived Cape & Natal Steam Nav. Co. The *Iceland* took her departure from Dartmouth on the 25 January 1872 but within a month the Cape &

Natal finally foundered and thus there came into being in 1876 the Castle Packets Co. which formally took over Currie's interests in the South African trade. A new mail contract in that same year was divided between the Union and Castle lines and eventually in 1881 the latter concern went public and was reorganised as the Castle Mail Packets Co. Ltd.

Contemporary Castle mail steamers included the 2820-ton *Dunrobin Castle*, completed by Robert Napier of Glasgow in 1876 and the first of a new generation of vessels designed especially for the Cape route, which in the course of her maiden voyage reduced the company's record for the passage by some twelve hours. This vessel was followed by the essentially similar *Balmoral Castle*, *Dublin Castle*, *Warwick Castle* and *Conway Castle*, all providing

(left) *Armand Behic* 1892 Messageries Maritimes. Built for the Australian and New Hebrides trade and named after a former chairman of the company. Photo: Author

(right) Triple expansion machinery permitted the use of higher steam pressures than hitherto and resulted in a considerable gain in fuel economy, the first vessel so fitted being the 3684-ton *Aberdeen* completed for Robert Napier for the Aberdeen Line in 1882. The tandem arrangement shown appeared somewhat later and proved popular for high powered merchant ships since the engine room length could be kept to a minimum.

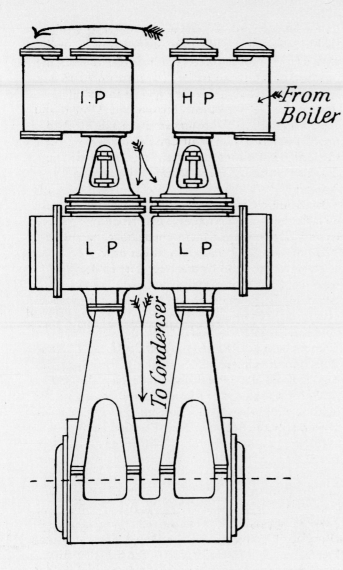

I.P   H P   *From Boiler*

L P   L P

To Condenser

accommodation for about 90 first and 50 second class passengers with facilities if required for the carriage of 100 emigrants in the cargo 'tween deck spaces. The *Dunrobin Castle* set the pattern for Castle steamers for several years; sturdy compound-engined vessels with a service speed of 12 to 14 knots, which formed the mainstay of the company's Cape mail trade until the advent of the 5625-ton Fairfield built *Dunottar Castle* in 1890.

In the meantime, early in 1877, the *Dunrobin Castle* had further reduced the record by steaming from Dartmouth to the Cape in 21 days 12 hours 49 minutes. This was bettered in the following October by the *Balmoral Castle* but after a brief taste of fame the record established by this latter vessel was decisively beaten by the Union Line steamer *German*, a 3028-ton compound engined vessel built by Denny of Dumbarton in that same year, 1877, which completed her passage out from Plymouth in 19 days 8½ hours. The rivalry between the two concerns was at this time intense extending to lengthy duels in the contemporary press. The 3199-ton *Pretoria* improved on the *German*'s time in October 1878 but there then followed a period of recession lasting until 1885 when the discovery of gold in the Witwatersrand completely transformed the South African economy. Hitherto, there had been little demand for emigrant steerage-style accommodation but with this new development the situation was radically changed overnight. Unlike other trades at this time, however, that with southern Africa involved largely the shipment out to the Cape of bulky engineering goods such as railway, dock and mining equipment, whereas homeward cargoes comprised primarily high-value bullion and gemstones of minimal bulk. Although it was the accepted practice in other trades to erect temporary accommodation for steerage traffic in the cargo 'tween deck spaces, in this case it failed to develop and instead the Castle Line introduced a definite third class in permanent accommodation. This first appeared in the 5625-ton *Dunottar Castle* of 1890 which provided for 160 first, 90 second and 100 third class passengers, with facilities for a further 150 'open berth' steerage passengers if required[6].

The *Dunottar Castle*, apart from any other consideration, was intended to break records and this she achieved in the course of her maiden voyage by steaming out from Dartmouth to the Cape in 17 days 19 hours 50 minutes. Her homeward passage was completed in 16 days 14 hours 15 minutes. The more conservative Union Line, which had long considered itself to be the premier concern catering in particular for the élite sector of the passenger trade, did little to encourage third class custom although limited provision was made in some vessels for emigrants in 'open berth' steerage accommodation. In fact, however, the time had come for some response on the part of the Union Line in the face of the policy of aggressive publicity adopted by their Castle rivals. Thus in July 1891 the former concern took delivery from Wm. Denny of that magnificent flyer, the 6844-ton clipper-stemmed *Scot* which in all probability never made a penny profit for the company! The first twin-screw steamer in the fleet, she was engined with triple expansion machinery and apart from other innovations was painted black with pale buff upperworks and yellow funnels, in contrast with the sombre overall black of earlier Union vessels.

The *Scot* first departed Southampton on the 25 July 1891 and arrived in Table Bay on the 10 August, cutting the passage time to under 15½ days. Having seized the initiative the Union Line took delivery in 1894 of the 7537-ton Belfast-built *Norman*. A two-funnelled vessel of conventional appearance, engined

with triple expansion machinery of 9000 ihp driving twin screws, she was a little slower than the *Scot* but with a service speed of 16 knots was able to work the outward passage via Madeira in a little under 16 days. Her accommodation was far superior to that of any other passenger vessel working out from United Kingdom ports, apart from certain North Atlantic liners, and the design of all Cape mail liners built for the Union and subsequently the Union-Castle Lines for the next fifteen years stemmed from that of the *Norman*.

In the meantime, electric lighting had replaced the oil lamps and candles which, apart from the abortive trials with gas lighting mentioned above, had provided the sole illumination in earlier days. As far back as 1879 the 5491-ton Inman liner *City of Berlin* had been fitted with six arc lamps in the dining saloon and engine/boiler rooms. Such installations were, however, little used for general shipboard lighting and not until the introduction in 1879 of the incandescent filament lamp, developed independently by Thomas Edison in the United States and by Joseph Swan in England, did electric lighting become a really practical proposition. One of Edison's first orders was for lighting equipment for a steamship named *Columbia*, presumably the 1468-ton New York-registered excursion vessel of that name built for the Rockaway Beach trade in 1877. Probably the first incandescent lighting installation in a British registered vessel was that fitted in 1880 in the 3847-ton Orient-Pacific liner *Chimborazo*, then employed in the Australian passenger trade. In November 1882, Wm. Denny of Dumbarton delivered the 1003-ton *Tarawera* (Union Steamship Co. of New Zealand), the first British registered merchant ship fitted throughout with '... Edison's incandescent electric light[7].' and by 1883

---

[6] Rhodes' Steamship Guide (1889–90) carried advertisements for the Castle and Union Line weekly services '... for the Gold Fields of South Africa.'

[7] *The Denny List* (National Maritime Museum, 1975). Yard No. 263.

such installations were being specified for the majority of new construction passenger steamships.

The 1880s were marked by the growth of foreign competition in the eastern and African trades bringing new problems for the established British overseas lines. Mention has been made already of the arrival of the Messageries Maritimes east of Suez, initially to the Far East and in 1882 to Australia and New Caledonia. Then in 1885 the Imperial German Government entered into an agreement with the Norddeutscher Lloyd whereby, in return for the award of a substantial subsidy, the company was to establish services to the Far East and Australasia. For these routes the company placed orders with AG Vulkan of Stettin for the construction of the 14-knot steel screw steamships *Preussen*, *Sachsen* and *Bayern*, all of which were delivered in 1886, the services having been inaugurated meanwhile by vessels transferred from the North and South Atlantic routes. Not all these vessels, particulary those designed for the cool North Atlantic climate, proved suited to service east of Suez, however, and not until 1889 when the company took steps to encourage growth of the passenger side of the business by the transfer of larger and more luxurious ships did the Norddeutscher Lloyd make any real impact in these trades.

Although United States operators showed relatively little interest in the Atlantic trade at this time, the well-found vessels of the Pacific Mail Steamship Co., trading between San Francisco and the Orient, and of the Oceanic Steam Ship Co. (Spreckel's Line), which worked via Honolulu to Australasia, provided a degree of comfort equal to the best available on other routes. Typical of the passenger vessels employed in the Pacific Australasian trade after the turn of the century were sisters *Sierra*, *Sonoma* and *Ventura*, twin-screw steamships built at Philadelphia by Wm. Cramp & Son and completed for service in 1900. Like many of their contemporaries they were fitted with refrigerating machinery for perishable stores, steam-driven plant of this type operating on the Linde ammonia cycle having been introduced for this purpose in about 1890.

Mention has been made already of the introduction in the 1880s of incandescent electric lighting which, in so far as passenger vessels were concerned, quickly displaced oil lamps and candles. Until the mid-1890s, however, little other use was found for electricity in merchant steamships apart from cabin call bells and simple forms of order telegraph equipment. Thus, the generators were small, being rated in terms of the number of lamps, usually of 16 candle power, that they were able to supply. For instance, the 12 950-ton Cunard record breaker *Campania* of 1893 was fitted with four Siemens HB 700 lamp dynamos operating at 80 volts direct current (dc), the total installed capacity being about 150 kilowatts. The introduction of electrically-driven ventilating fans in about 1898 marked, however, the beginning of the widespread adoption of electricity for auxiliary plant, space-heating and galley equipment in passenger steamships, and within a few years its use was to have a profound influence on the degree of comfort provided for travellers other than those confined to the lower grade third class and steerage accommodation.

In the meantime, United States' interests had been buying their way into the North Atlantic passenger trade in the guise of the International Navigation Co. The company started in Philadelphia in 1873 with the Red Star Line worked by a Belgian flag subsidiary, but in due course it acquired the British flag Inman Line and eventually, after the turn of the century, the Leyland, White Star, Atlantic Transport and Dominion Lines. Reorganised in 1902 as the International Mercantile Marine Co., the group promoted the White Star Line as its leading contender for the cream of the Atlantic passenger traffic, although the fleet retained its British registry. For twenty years the White Star had vied with Cunard, Inman and others for the Atlantic 'Blue Riband', but in the wake of the entry into service in 1899 of the 17 274-ton *Oceanic* the company had withdrawn from the race having opted instead for a policy involving the construction of large comfortable vessels of moderate speed. The 19-knot *Oceanic* was the last of the Harland & Wolff 'long ships' but she was no record-breaker, the credit for the fastest passage having been claimed already by the Norddeutscher Lloyd's

Kaiser Wilheim der Grosse which crossed from Sandy Hook to the Needles in November 1897 at an average speed of 22.35 knots.

The first vessel designed in keeping with the new White Star policy, the 20 904-ton *Celtic*, was delivered by Harland & Wolff in July 1901. At the time of her completion the new vessel was the largest afloat, but with a service speed of no more than $16\frac{1}{2}$ knots she represented a radical new approach to ocean travel combining spacious comfort with economy of operation. Accommodation was provided for 347 first class, 160 second class and no fewer than 2352 third class passengers, the latter in considerably greater comfort than was the usual practice at the time. There

Teutonic 1889 White Star Line. The last of the White Star record–breakers and the first North Atlantic liner to be built for rapid conversion as an armed merchant cruiser in time of war. Photo: B. Feilden

was in addition stowage for some 17000 tons of cargo, although it must have been something of a problem to make the best use of such capacity in a vessel tied to a strict schedule. The *Celtic* was followed by three near sisters and within the next few years the Hamburg-Amerika Linie and the Norddeutscher Lloyd, both of which had working agreements with the International Mercantile Marine Co., built a series of similar vessels. All proved steady dividend earners.

On the 26 June 1897 the crowd assembled for the Queen's Diamond Jubilee Review of the Fleet at Spithead witnessed the first public, if unofficial, demonstration of the potential of the marine steam turbine when Sir Charles Parsons' yacht *Turbinia* streaked at 34 knots across the Solent. In the event, one Captain John Williamson formed Turbine

Steamers Ltd. and entered into an agreement with the Dumbarton shipbuilders Wm. Denny & Bros. and the Parsons Marine Steam Turbine Co. which resulted in the construction in 1901 of the 551-ton Clyde ferry steamer *King Edward*. Fitted with direct-drive turbines on three shafts (until 1905 there were two screws on each of the wing shafts) the *King Edward* was capable of 19 knots and proved an immediate success on the Fairlie to Campbeltown service for which she had been designed. She was to remain in service until 1951, latterly on the Glasgow to the Arran coast run.

Refrigerating arrangements in the White Star liner *Teutonic* of 1890. The refrigerating machinery and cold rooms were sited between and below the two propeller shafts. ('North Atlantic Ferry', 1892.)

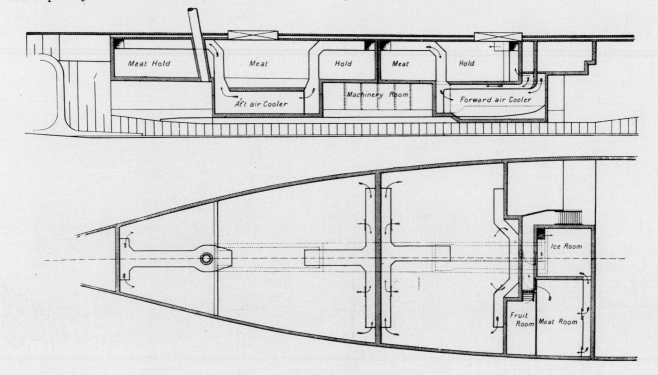

The *King Edward* amply demonstrated the lack of vibration associated with the steam turbine machinery and in October 1903 the Glasgow-based Allan Line announced that orders had been placed for a pair of 18-knot triple-screw turbine steamers for the Canadian trade. First to enter service was the 10635-ton *Victorian* which took her maiden sailing from Liverpool on the 25 August 1905. At about the same time Cunard appointed a working party to look into the desirability, or otherwise, of adopting turbine machinery for a projected pair of 24½-knot express steamships for the North Atlantic crossing. Before coming to a firm decision, however, the company decided to fit turbines in the second of two intermediate liners then under construction at Clydebank. The vessel concerned, the 19524-ton *Carmania*,

entered service on the Liverpool to New York route in December 1905 by which time a decision in favour of turbine machinery had been made in the case of the new vessels for the weekly express service.

The Cunard contracts were placed in May 1905 and on the 7 June 1906 the *Lusitania* entered the water at Clydebank. As completed in September 1907 she was at 30396 gross tons the world's largest vessel,

(right) *Lusitania* 1907 Cunard Line. The 31550-ton turbine-engined express liner which brought the North Atlantic record back to Cunard after a break of 13 years. Photo: Author

(below) *Canada* 1896 Dominion Line. Built expressly for the St. Lawrence trade and easily the finest of the Dominion Line steamships. Photo: B.Feilden

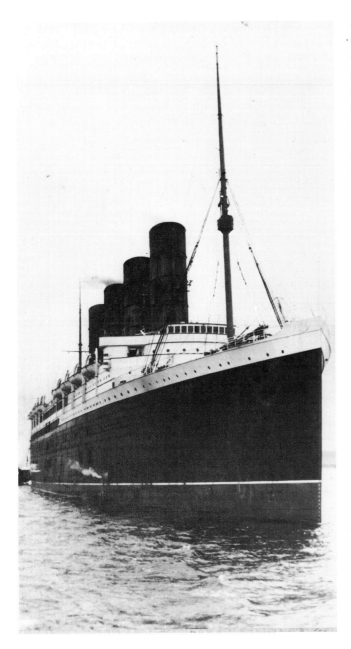

with provision for 552 first, 460 second and 1186 third class passengers. Her first class public rooms were decorated and furnished on a truly magnificent scale representing the peak of Edwardian splendour, and the vessel soon acquired a reputation for comfort and seaworthiness. With her four naked funnels and clean lines she and her sister, the Tyne-built *Mauretania*, were supreme examples of the shipbuilder's art in an age when ocean travel was becoming increasingly popular. The electric generating plant, with an installed capacity of 1500 kilowatts, or ten times that of the *Campania* completed only fourteen years earlier, provided power for deck machinery, the refrigeration plant, galley equipment, ventilation fans, ash hoists, passenger lifts and space-heating.

In the course of her second voyage in October 1907 the *Lusitania* took the North Atlantic 'Blue Riband' in both directions from the Norddeutscher Lloyd's *Kaiser Wilhelm II* and thus brought back to Cunard the record which was to be retained for no less than 22 years, until July 1929 when the *Mauretania* finally conceded the honour to the Norddeutscher Lloyd's newly-completed express liner *Bremen*.

The White Star Line and the Hamburg-Amerika Linie kept, in so far as their premier North Atlantic services were concerned, to a policy of building large comfortable vessels of moderate speed. In the meantime, however, in 1909 Messrs. Harland & Wolff had completed for the White Star Canadian service the 14 892-ton triple-screw liner *Laurentic* engined with triple expansion machinery on the two outer shafts exhausting into a low pressure turbine directly coupled to the centre screw. Combination machinery of this type, which had first appeared in the New Zealand Shipping Co's. cargo liner *Otaki* completed at Belfast in 1908, was chosen for the first of the White Star giants, the 45 324-ton *Olympic* delivered by Harland & Wolff in June 1911 for the company's premier Southampton to New York service.

Compared with the *Lusitania* and *Mauretania* the design of the Olympic was, apart from the matter of sheer size, somewhat conventional although in order to achieve the desired strength the hull scantlings were exceptionally heavy. The White Star 'Big Four' *Celtic*, *Cedric*, *Baltic* and *Adriatic*, had each been in turn the world's largest ship and now this honour passed to the *Olympic*. Accommodation was provided for 689 first, 674 second and 1026 third class passengers, 164 of the latter even at this late day being in open berths. The first class accommodation amidships could only be described as magnificent and apart from the superb public rooms, included Turkish baths, a swimming pool and squash courts. Designed for a service of 21 knots, the *Olympic* was the first of an intended trio for her owners' weekly service to New York and proved immediately popular. In the event, disaster overtook the *Titanic* in 1912 whilst the *Britannic*, hastily completed for service as a hospital ship in December 1915, was mined and sunk in the Aegean only eleven months later!

The Hamburg-Amerika Linie, pursuing a similar policy to that of the White Star Line, placed an order with AG Vulkan of Hamburg in the early summer of 1910 for the first of a trio of giant vessels for the company's New York service which, with calls at Southampton and Cherbourg, would be in direct competition with the White Star on the Atlantic crossing. Completed for service in June 1913, the 51969-ton

Imperator had little of the grace of the White Star and Cunard express liners, an impression which was not helped by the enormous bronze eagle which adorned her stem. Engined with Parsons turbines built under licence by AG Vulkan, she was designed for 23 knots but stability problems marred her early days and not until the overburden of topweight had been reduced following a serious fire in New York did she prove satisfactory in North Atlantic service. Accommodation for no fewer than 4234 passengers, together

Titanic 1912 White Star Line. Foundered with the loss of 1503 lives after striking an iceberg four days out from Southampton on her maiden voyage. Photo: NMM

with a crew numbering 1180, created in the wake of the *Titanic* disaster a problem in so far as the provision of sufficient boats was concerned but this was eventually overcome by arranging the stowages on two decks. There were 83 boats in all!

Cunard completed its plans for a three-ship Liverpool to New York weekly express service with the delivery in May 1914 of the 45 647-ton *Aquitania*. Designed for 23 knots she was no record-breaker. On the other hand she proved sea-kindly, whilst the superb luxury of her first class accommodation brought immediate popularity although she completed but three round voyages before the outbreak of the First World War completely disrupted the North Atlantic passenger trade. Fortunately, the *Aquitania* was to survive both World Wars, and was finally sold for breaking up at Faslane in February 1950. In the course of 36 years service she had steamed some three million miles and had carried nearly 1.2 million passengers. All in all she probably represents the best investment that Cunard ever made, since she was built without the aid of any government loan or other subvention.

In the meantime, the construction of the Clyde turbine steamer *King Edward* had been followed in 1902 by an order placed with the same builders, Wm. Denny & Bros., by the South Eastern & Chatham Railway for a triple-screw turbine vessel for the Dover/Folkestone short sea services. Launched as *The Queen*, this 1676-ton steamer entered service in 1903 and quickly established a reputation for comfort, reliability and economy. With her two funnels, elliptical stern and clean lines she set the pattern for vessels intended for the short sea crossing to France for the next 15 years. Direct drive turbine machinery was not adopted for the longer overnight crossings for which speed was not such an important consideration and for some years more these routes continued to be served by reciprocating engined screw steamers such as the 2254-ton *Patriotic* built in 1911 for the Liverpool to Belfast trade of the Belfast Steamship Co. In November of that same year, however, the London & South Western Railway Co. took delivery of the 1560-ton Fairfield-built *Normannia*, the first passenger engined with Parsons geared turbines. Machinery of this type, with its lower propeller speeds and relative freedom from vibration, proved ideal for medium-powered installations intended for the longer overnight crossings demanding service speeds of 16 to 19 knots and it was widely adopted for the next generation of vessels designed for these cross-channel and near continental routes.

Short sea passenger vessels intended for operation on the Canadian eastern seaboard or for Australian and New Zealand waters, designed and in most cases built in United Kingdom shipyards, bore a marked similarity to those engaged in the home-based trades. Elsewhere, however, distinctive features were evolved to suit local conditions. In particular the American steamers built for the Puget Sound trade were distinguished by their broad low hulls surmounted by a long wooden superstructure housing the staterooms, the latter arranged either side of the long narrow saloon as had long been the practice in American river steamers. Similar features marked the design of the Pacific coast steamers of the Canadian Pacific Railway Co. built for the Vancouver–Victoria–Seattle 'Triangle' trade. Typical of these craft was the 1943 ton twin-screw steamer *Princess Victoria*, launched by Swan Hunter at Newcastle in November 1902. Designed for a service speed of 19 knots, she was engined with triple expansion machinery and steamed out to the Pacific via the Straits of Magellan minus her wooden superstructure, completing the passage without incident in 59 days. The *Princess Victoria* was followed in 1908 by the 3925-ton *Princess Charlotte* and in 1910 by the 3061-ton *Princess Adelaide*, both built at Govan by Fairfield. However, the outbreak of war overtook the construction of the *Princess Irene* and *Princess Margaret*, geared turbine steamers of 5900 gross tons apiece, orders for which had been placed with Wm. Denny in May 1913. Taken over by the Royal Navy and completed as minelayers they were never to see service on the 'Triangle' route for which they had been designed.

By August 1914 when war erupted in Europe the evolution of the passenger steamship was practically complete. In matters of luxury and comfort, accommodation standards now mirrored the best to be found on shore and future changes, apart from the introduction between the wars of new propulsion machinery, were to be confined to a trend towards ever-increasing size together with alterations in outward appearance to suit prevailing fashion.

Normannia 1911 London & South Western Rly. Co. The first geared turbine-engined passenger steamship. Employed on the Southampton to Le Havre route. Photo: NMM

Between the Wars

In the aftermath of war shipowners sought first to rebuild their fleets whilst taking stock of future trends in world trade. To some extent, gaps in the fleets of the western allies were made good by the acquisition of German vessels handed over under the terms of the peace treaty, among others being the HAPAG liner *Imperator* which became the Cunard *Berengaria*. Doubts about US immigration policy resulted in caution on the part of shipowners in so far as the North Atlantic trade was concerned, however, and new construction orders were for medium sized vessels of moderate speed such as the 19 730 ton *Scythia*, completed for Cunard by Vickers (Barrow) in August 1921. Engined with double-reduction geared turbine machinery, she was designed for a service speed of 16 knots and provided accommodation for 350 first, 350 second and 1500 third class passengers.

The *Scythia* was followed by four similar vessels for the Liverpool to New York trade and in May 1922 Cunard took delivery of the 13 950-ton *Andania*, the first of six smaller 15-knot vessels designed for the Canadian services with accommodation for 500 cabin-class[8] and 1200 third class passengers. Similar vessels were built also for the associated Anchor and Anchor-Donaldson Lines.

Requirements for the South African trade differed considerably from those of the North Atlantic. The Union Castle Mail Steamship Co. worked a weekly service to the Cape leaving Southampton every Friday at 4 pm and was in the fortunate position that its mail fleet survived the war without loss, although the veteran *Norman* (1894) and *Briton* (1897) were obviously due for retirement. A replacement for the former had been laid down in 1915 but it was in September 1919 before she was launched as *Arundel Castle*. A coal-burning steamship of 18 980 tons, she retained the pre-war class structure and provided accommodation for 234 first, 362 second, 274 third class and 300 steerage passengers. In appearance she was decidedly old fashioned, for, although given a cruiser stern she had four tall thin funnels, the after one a dummy.

In the course of their post-war refits many vessels, particularly those employed on the North Atlantic, were converted from coal- to oil-burning, thereby reducing considerably the demand for labour for firing the boilers. New construction vessels were in most cases oil-fired but on the other hand many companies, such as the Peninsular & Oriental, with large fleets working east of Suez, continued to specify steam reciprocating machinery, since the tight interlocking schedule of services in eastern waters demanded maximum reliability. In Britain this policy was considered by many to be a retrograde step but in fact a number of operators were looking to the internal combustion diesel engine as the propulsion plant of the future. Already the Danish East Asiatic Co. and the Glen Line had considerable operating experience with diesel-engined vessels, but now the Royal Mail group under the leadership of Sir Owen Philipps, later Lord Kylsant, committed itself completely to propulsion plant of this type.

[8] Previously known on the North Atlantic as Second Class.

In 1927, the Royal Mail group included, among others, the Pacific Steam Nav. Co., the Union Castle Mail Steamship Co., Elder Dempster, the White Star Line and the Nelson Steam Nav. Co., on whose behalf orders were placed with Harland & Wolff for a series of twin-screw passenger motor vessels as planned fleet replacements. These ships varied in size from the 9333-ton *Apapa*, completed in 1927 for Elder Dempster's Liverpool–West Africa trade, to the 27759-ton *Georgic* delivered in 1932 for the White Star Line's secondary North Atlantic service from Liverpool. All exhibited features in common such as cruiser-style sterns and short squat funnels with the tops cut parallel to the waterline. In all but the Elder Dempster vessels the masts and funnels were heavily raked, and it is interesting to note that similar characteristics marked the profile of the 3737-ton motor vessel *Ulster Monarch*, and her sisters, completed by Harland & Wolff for the Liverpool to Belfast service of the Belfast Steamship Co. in 1929.

Among the first to adopt diesel propulsion for its main line passenger service had been the German Hamburg-Sud Amerika Linie which in November 1924 took delivery of the 13625-ton *Monte Sarmiento*, the first of a series of similar vessels for the River Plate trade all providing accommodation for large numbers of third class (subsequently tourist) and steerage passengers only. Swedish owners, too, placed orders for diesel-engined passenger vessels, and in November 1927 Ansaldo SA of Sestri Ponente delivered to the Navagazione Generale Italiana the 32650-ton *Augustus*, then the largest motor ship afloat and, in the event, the largest-ever passenger vessel with machinery of this type.

Protagonists of the diesel engine claimed a number of advantages including a considerably better power/weight ratio and reduced manning requirements when compared with steam plant of comparable output. On the other hand, diesel fuel was more expensive than furnace fuel oils but against this could be set the greater economy of the internal combustion engine and a reduction in the space devoted to bunkers.

Berengaria 1913 Cunard Line. Built as the HAPAG *Imperator* but surrendered to Britain and purchased as a replacement for the Cunard *Lusitania*. Photographed in dock at Southampton. Photo: Author

Carinthia 1925 Cunard Line. Similar to the *Scythia* of 1921 but redesigned internally with improved accommodation for winter cruising. Employed also on the Liverpool to New York service. Photo: B.Feilden

These early marine diesel engines were large, slow running and fitted for reversing, the crankshaft being directly coupled via the thrust block to the propeller.

In the event, the diesel engine proved particularly suited to the needs of the passenger vessel designed for a service speed in the range of 14 to 18 knots. The well-proven triple or quadruple expansion engine retained its popularity, however, for lower powered vessels of under 10 000 gross tons, such as the 8139-ton *Yoma* completed by Wm Denny for the Rangoon trade of the Glasgow based Henderson Line in 1928, whilst for high powered craft, in particular those intended for the short sea crossings, the geared turbine with its marked freedom from vibration offered the best choice.

Developed initially in the United States, electric transmission offered a viable alternative to mechanical reduction gearing for turbine driven steamships. The steam turbine itself is, of course, non-reversing and among other advantages claimed was that the employment of electric transmission not only made unnecessary the provision of an astern turbine, but also that full power could be made available both ahead and astern. Among the first to adopt turbo-electric propulsion for passenger steamships was the Peninsular & Oriental S.N. Co. which in February 1929 accepted

Georgic 1932 White Star Line. 27759 tons. The largest British diesel-engined passenger liner and the last vessel built for the White Star Line. Photo: B.Feilden

delivery for its London to Bombay service of the 19648-ton *Viceroy of India*, a 19-knot vessel providing accommodation for 415 first and 258 second class passengers. Apart from her machinery installation she was an enlarged, faster version of the reciprocating engined *Ranpura* class completed for the Bombay trade in 1925.

Increasingly restrictive immigration policies, cut-throat competition and generally depressed trading conditions in the late 1920s brought about considerable changes in the passenger class structure. Other than in the South American trade, steerage accommodation had all but disappeared; now the old second class and the better end of the third class (cabin) accommodation were assimilated in a new tourist class which eventually displaced all secondary grades other than 'dormitory' (steerage) accommodation.

In the meantime, in July 1929, the Norddeutscher Lloyd had marked its recovery from the ravages of war by regaining the North Atlantic Blue Riband held since 1907 by the Cunard veteran *Mauretania*. The 51656-ton *Bremen*, and her sister the 49746-ton *Europa*, were designed for a service speed of 27 knots with a bid for Atlantic supremacy in mind and were

intended to work with the 32565-ton *Columbus*, a former triple expansion engined vessel dating from 1923 now re-engined with geared turbine machinery. In appearance too, the *Columbus* was rebuilt to resemble the long low silhouette of the *Bremen* and *Europa* with two squat buff funnels, the tops of which were cut parallel to the waterline like those of contemporary Harland & Wolff motor vessels. However, she did retain her outmoded counter stern and thus could easily be distinguished from her consorts. An innovation in the *Bremen* and *Europa* was the provision of an aircraft catapult and a Heinkel floatplane enabling the mails to be forwarded when the ship was still some 600 miles from her destination. The French Line (Compagnie Générale Transatlantique) express liner *Ile de France* (43153 tons) was similarly fitted.

At this time, the Cunard express service from Southampton was being worked by an ageing, albeit popular, trio comprising the *Mauretania*, *Aquitania* and *Berengaria* (ex *Imperator*). Forced to look to its laurels in the wake of the advent of the *Bremen*, the company announced in May 1930 the placing of an order with John Brown & Co. of Clydebank for the construction of the first of two express liners which it

Ben-my-Chree 1927 Isle of Man Steam Pkt. Co. A 2586-ton twin screw geared turbine steamer built for the summer seasonal services from Liverpool and Fleetwood to the Isle of Man. Photo: B.Feilden

was intended should eventually replace the existing trio. The keel of Yard No. 534 was laid in December 1930 but a stoppage of two years and more resulting from the world wide depression delayed her launch until the 29 September 1934 when she entered the water as *Queen Mary*. Completed in May 1936 the new contender for the Atlantic crown was a quadruple-screw geared turbine engined vessel of 80 774 tons providing accommodation for 776 cabin (first class), 784 tourist and 579 third class passengers. There were no startling innovations and the *Queen Mary* was essentially a larger, faster up-dated version of the *Aquitania* which in the course of 31 years service was to prove a magnificent asset to both her owners and the nation.

The French Line (Compagnie Generale Transatlantique) too had made plans for re-vitalising its North Atlantic express service and towards the end of 1930, in the wake of the Cunard order for Yard No. 534, a contract was placed with the Chantiers et Ateliers de St. Nazaire for a vessel 1029 feet long which was to outclass all others afloat. Delivered in May 1935, the 79 280-ton *Normandie* displayed no obvious parentage whilst her fine lines from the gracefully curved stem and turtle-backed forecastle to the rounded semi-counter stern, were exceptionally clean and, with the three streamlined funnels, pleasing to the eye. The decor of the public rooms was in keeping with the 'art deco' idiom of the 1930s and a far cry from the plastic and chrome decoration of contemporary German liners or the baroque interiors of the Italian *Rex* and *Conte di Savoia*. The *Normandie* took her first sailing from Le Havre on the 29 May 1935 and broke all existing records with an average of 29.98 knots outwards and 30.35 knots in the homeward direction.

Queen Mary 1936 Cunard–White Star Ltd. Laid down for Cunard as the first of two express steamships for the weekly Southampton to New York service but completed in the name of Cunard–White Star. She remains afloat as a museum, hotel ship and convention centre at Long Beach, California. Photo: B.Feilden

In other trades also the trend throughout the 1930s was towards faster mail and passenger services worked by fewer ships. Thus in March 1936 in preparation for the introduction of an accelerated service to the Cape, the Union Castle Mail Steamship Co. embarked upon an ambitious programme involving the reconstruction of five vessels of its mail fleet to enable them to work alongside the 20-knot motor ships *Stirling Castle* and *Athlone Castle* orders for which had been placed with Harland & Wolff in February 1934. In so far as the *Arundel Castle*, *Windsor Castle* and *Carnarvon Castle* were concerned, the work involved not only the fitting of new higher powered machinery but also lengthening to improve the hull form. It is a tribute to all concerned that the mammoth task was completed on time and in particular the *Arundel Castle* and *Windsor Castle* emerged as magnificent two-funneled vessels with graceful curved stems, their pleasing lines being well set off by their lavender grey hulls and black topped red funnels.

For the Australian trade the Peninsular & Oriental took delivery in 1931/32 of the 22 450-ton turbo-electric sister ships *Strathnaver* and *Strathaird* which, in place of the traditional black with stone coloured upperworks, were painted white with yellow funnels. Of the three funnels, the forward and after were dummies which in itself generated a problem since the middle funnel quickly became discoloured in service! The sisters were intended for an accelerated 19-knot mail service, although they could maintain 21 knots if required.

The Peninsular & Oriental appears never to have been really convinced by the arguments in favour of a turbo-electric drive and for its next generation of passenger vessels the company adopted single reduction geared turbine machinery. Similar in appearance to the turbo-electric 'Straths' but with only a single funnel, the 23 580-ton *Strathmore* entered service in 1935 although it was October 1937 before she joined her consorts in the Australian trade working out from Tilbury to Bombay, Colombo, Adelaide, Melbourne and Sydney. Fortnightly sailings alternated with those of the associated Orient Line although the latter company's vessels omitted the call at Bombay and instead worked through to Brisbane.

An interesting facet of the close P&O/Orient ties in the 1930s was the adoption of common designs in so far as vessels intended for the Australian trade were concerned. Thus the hull design and geared turbine machinery installation of the 23 371-ton *Orion*, which entered Orient Line service in September 1935, was practically identical to that of the *Strathmore* although in so far as outward appearances were concerned the two vessels had little in common. The *Orion* was given

a corn coloured hull with green boot topping and with her buff cowl topped funnel and single mast quickly earned a nick-name in Sydney as the 'Big Tug'. She provided accommodation for 486 first and 653 tourist class passengers and among other innovations certain of the public rooms were air-conditioned.

The trade which generated probably the fiercest competition in the 1930s was that between Europe and the east coast of South America which comprised not only routine business traffic but also the carriage

Orcades 1937 Orient Steam Nav. Co. In 1935, the Orient Line adopted for new construction a distinctive and undoubtedly attractive livery comprising a corn–coloured hull, green boot topping and white upperworks whilst retaining the earlier yellow cowl topped funnel. Photo: Author

annually of many hundreds of emigrants. French, German, Italian and British companies were involved but it was a trade which the Germans, and subsequently the French, tried to make their own. The Hamburg-Sud Amerika Linie, in October 1927, took delivery of the 27 560-ton twin-screw geared turbine steamship *Cap Arcona*, a 21-knot vessel providing accommodation for 575 first, 275 second and 465 third class passengers although in the event she proved too large for the trade. Not to be outdone, the Cie. de Nav. Sud Atlantique went to Penhoët with the order for an even larger vessel which was delivered in September 1931 as *L'Atlantique*, a 42 512-ton geared turbine steamship with accommodation for 414 first, 158 second and 584 third class passengers. Like the

Cap Arcona she proved too big and probably her owners were not too upset when she caught fire while underway without passengers from Bordeaux to Le Havre for docking on the 4 January 1934. Following a long court case she was abandoned to the underwriters eventually to be sold for breaking up on the Clyde.

For many years United States Lines, the US North Atlantic flag carrier, struggled to make a profit. In the

America 1940 United States Lines. An improved *Manhattan* built for the New York to Southampton and Le Havre service as a replacement for the ex-German *Leviathan*. The outbreak of war in Europe delayed her maiden North Atlantic sailing until November 1946. Photo: Author

wake of a disastrous start in the 1920s with a fleet comprising a miscellaneous assortment of ex-German liners and former US Army transports, the company built the 24 289-ton twin-screw geared turbine sisters *Manhattan* and *Washington* which entered service in August 1932 and May 1933, respectively. For a time these two vessels worked in company with the 48 943-ton *Leviathan*, formerly the HAPAG *Vaterland*, but this 'white elephant' was laid up in 1935 when the company undertook to build a third, improved, vessel of the *Manhattan* type. Launched as *America* on the 31 August 1939 this 26 454-ton[9] geared turbine steamship was completed in July 1940 by which time Europe

had gone to war and there was no longer any North Atlantic passenger trade other than traffic generated by the needs of war. In the absence of other employment she was diverted to cruising until taken up for fitting out as a troop transport in 1941.

The war escalated into a global conflict and one by one the world's passenger liners were diverted to naval or military service. Many were to be destroyed and not until 1945 were any of the survivors to be returned to their owners.

[9] When re-measured in 1946 the gross tonnage of the *America* was assessed at 33 532 tons.

Nieuw Amsterdam 1938 Nederlandsch-Amerikaansche S.M. 36 287 tons. Built for the Rotterdam to New York service of the Holland America Line (N.A.S.M.). As completed her hull was painted black with a gilt riband. Photo: Author

Post War and decline

Although the war in Europe ended on the 8 May 1945 and that in the Far East some 14 weeks later, many months passed before the surviving passenger liners were handed back to their owners. Refitting of those fit for further service occupied months more, and it was 1948 before any semblance of the pre-war pattern of services began to take shape. In the meantime the remaining German passenger vessels had been distributed among the allies whilst of the Japanese merchant fleet little remained to be claimed as the spoils of war.

At an early stage, however, British owners in particular gave thought to future needs and in the event a number of prominent companies, including Cunard-White Star, the Shaw, Savill & Albion Co., Alfred Holt & Co., the Blue Star Line and the Cie. Maritime Belge, opted for the construction of medium-sized passenger-cargo liners with accommodation for between 30 and 250 first class passengers only. Typical of this group, the 15 902-twin-screw geared turbine steamship *Athenic* was completed by Harland & Wolff for the New Zealand trade of the Shaw, Savill & Albion Co. in July 1947. This 17-knot vessel provided accommodation for 85 first-class passengers and with her sisters *Corinthic*, *Ceramic* and *Gothic* worked out from London via the Panama Canal to New Zealand ports.

A markedly different policy was adopted by, among others, the Peninsular & Oriental, the Orient Line, the Union Castle Mail Steamship Co. and the Soc. Gen. des Transports Maritimes, all of whom embarked upon the construction of larger, faster developments of pre-war designs in anticipation of a further acceleration of their premier services. In the case of the 18 705-ton Union Castle sisters *Edinburgh Castle* and *Pretoria Castle*, completed in 1948, this involved a reversion to geared turbine machinery since diesel engines of adequate power for 22 knots were not available in Britain. It is interesting to note, however, that the sisters *Giulio Cesare* and *Augustus*, vessels of similar size and speed completed for the Genoa to the River Plate service of the 'Italia' Line in the early 1950s, were engined with Fiat diesels of 35 000 bhp driving twin screws.

In so far as the North Atlantic trade between European ports and New York was concerned, the economic limits of speed and size had been reached in the design of the immediate pre-war express liners and new construction comprised mainly vessels of moderate dimensions and speed such as the 20 464-ton *Flandre*, which although intended originally for the Caribbean trade of the Cie. Générale Transatlantique was first employed in the New York service working alongside the *Liberté* (formerly the Norddeutscher Lloyd's *Europa*) and the ageing *Ile de France*. Engined with double-reduction geared turbine machinery, the 22-knot *Flandre* entered service in July 1952 but, unfortunately, her maiden voyage was marred by mechanical and electrical breakdowns and eventually she reached New York in tow! Ten years later she left the North Atlantic to join her sister the 19 828-ton *Antilles* in the West Indies trade for which she had been designed.

The post-war passenger boom reached its zenith in

the summer of 1950 when Cunard-White Star was employing no fewer than nine vessels in the New York Trade alone, in addition to four working out from Southampton to Canadian ports. The boom lasted through Coronation year 1953 and for a few years more but from 1960, in the wake of the introduction of large jet aircraft, there was a progressive decline in the numbers of passengers carried by sea.

In the meantime, it had become clear that the carriage of passengers and large cargoes in the same vessel was not an entirely satisfactory arrangement since circumstances outside the owner's control frequently resulted in delays in turn round and the consequent disruption of advertised schedules. Thus when the question of fleet replacements for the older units of the Shaw, Savill & Albion fleet came up it was decided that the needs of both shippers and passengers would best be served by the divorce of their opposing interests and the construction of a ship devoted entirely to the transit of passengers. In keeping with this new policy the company placed an order with Harland & Wolff for the construction of a 20 200-ton 20-knot geared turbine steamship to be named *Southern Cross*. The layout of the passenger decks and public rooms was greatly facilitated by the absence of cargo hatches and by the fact that the machinery,

Parthia 1948 Cunard–White Star Ltd. The second of two passenger cargo steamships built for the Liverpool to New York service in the aftermath of World War Two. Accommodation was provided for 250 first class passengers only. Photo: B. Feilden

together with the associated uptakes and downtakes, was positioned well aft. In keeping with the current trend, provision was made for 1160 one-class passengers in fully air-conditioned accommodation, whilst Denny-Brown stabilisers were fitted to minimise rolling in heavy weather.

The *Southern Cross* entered service in February 1955 on a new round-the-world route working out from Southampton via Panama to Wellington, Sydney, Melbourne, Fremantle, Durban, Capetown and thus via the Canary Islands back to Southampton, the passage time being 76 days. It was intended that the vessel should be considered as a sea-going hotel catering both for regular business and holiday traffic. In the event, the concept proved successful and in 1959 an order was placed with Vickers-Armstrongs

(Tyne) for the construction of a consort which was launched in June 1961 as *Northern Star*. Completed in July 1962 this second vessel entered service on an east-about route and it is interesting to note that the two ships between them were able to provide eight round-the-world sailings (four in each direction) per year with an annual passenger capacity very little less than that of the eleven passenger vessels comprising the combined Shaw, Savill & Albion and Aberdeen & Commonwealth fleets in 1939!

Himalaya 1949 Peninsular & Oriental S.N.Co. 27 955 tons. The second of six similar vessels built for the Australian services of the P&O and Orient Lines between 1948 and 1954. Photo: Author

The P&O-Orient combine had introduced a round-the-world service in 1958 by which time, however, it was apparent that the construction of further vessels of the immediate post-war *Himalaya* type would be uneconomic since the outlay involved would be too great in relation to their earning potential. It was decided instead that the answer lay in the construction of larger, faster ships which would not only enable the company to provide an accelerated Australian service but would permit also the introduction of a fast Pacific service. The two companies, although linked financially, were otherwise still relatively independent and the two new vessels built, one for each houseflag, in pursuance of the new policy, were markedly dissimilar apart from the fact that both were designed for

a service speed of 27 knots. The 41 923-ton *Oriana*, completed for the Orient Line by Vickers-Armstrongs (Barrow) in November 1960 was a more-or-less conventional but essentially reliable twin-screw, double-reduction geared turbine steamship with an out-dated direct current electrical system. The 45 270-ton Belfast-built *Canberra* represented a further development in the engines aft concept. Once again, the P&O turned to turbo-electric propulsion although, in the event, lack of recent experience in the design of this type of equipment did give rise to serious problems before the vessel settled down to the service for which she had been built. In addition to the now customary air-conditioning and stabilisers, the *Canberra* was fitted with a bow thruster to facilitate berthing whilst her alternating current electrical system was relatively new to British merchant ship practice.

By this time the North Atlantic race was over. In June 1952, United States Lines had taken delivery of the 53 329-ton *United States* built at Newport News on behalf of the US Government and designed at the height of the Korean War for rapid conversion as a military transport. She took her maiden sailing from New York on the 3 July 1952 and secured the east-

Canberra 1961 Peninsular & Oriental S.N.Co. 45 270 tons. Designed to partner the 41 915-ton *Oriana* in the P&O Orient Lines Australian and trans-Pacific services.

bound record for all time at an average speed of 35.39 knots. Engined with Westinghouse geared turbines developing a total of 240 000 shp, this quadruple-screw vessel achieved a speed of 38.32 knots during contractor's sea trials but against this must be set the fact that she had not been designed with the economics of the North Atlantic passenger trade in mind. Designed with a view to keeping fire risks to a minimum the use of wood was virtually eliminated, all furnishings and decorations being of fire retardant materials. In all, the *United States* cost nearly 70 000 000 dollars to build but she was 'sold' to United States Lines for 32 000 000 dollars.

The final group of passenger liners built especially for the North Atlantic trade comprised the magnificent *France*, a 66 348-ton geared turbine steamship completed for the Cie. Générale Transatlantique in January 1962, and the 45 900-ton 'Italia' Line sisters *Michelangelo* and *Raffaello*, completed in 1965. In all three vessels fresh attempts were made to prevent the deposition of soot on the passenger decks by careful attention to funnel design, in the case of the *France* by passing the furnace gases out via aerofoil 'wings' on either side of the two funnels and in the Italian vessels by fitting flared cowls to the funnels in order to induce an updraught. All three vessels were superbly elegant examples of the naval architect's art, but their construction was only made possible by the award of large subsidies by the governments concerned.

To the business world, time means money and already by 1960 the bulk of this traffic was being handled by air. In that year nearly 2 000 000 passengers crossed the North Atlantic by air compared with the 858 000 who, with time to spare, travelled by sea. The writing was indeed on the wall in so far as the scheduled passenger services were concerned and to an ever-increasing extent suitable vessels were diverted to cruising in order to satisfy a growing leisure market. Others either too large for cruising, too old or just not taken up for further service under the 'convenience' flags of Liberia or Panama, went to breakers in Spain, Hong Kong or Taiwan.

The last passenger vessel built for the Cape trade of the Union Castle Mail Steamship Co., the 32 697-ton *Transvaal Castle*, entered service in January 1932. A twin-screwed geared turbine steamship with provision for 728 one class passengers, she was transferred in January 1966 to the associated South African Marine Corporation (Safmarine) and renamed *SA Vaal* although she retained her United Kingdom registry

until February 1969. In this guise on the 2 September 1977 she took the last sailing in the joint Union Castle/Safmarine service to the Cape thus effectively putting a period to the story of the passenger liner.

France 1962 Cie. Générale Transatlantique. Built for the CGT with substantial government assistance and one of the last great North Atlantic liners. Photo: French Line

The withdrawal of scheduled services on the ocean routes was accompanied by the demise of the conventional passenger steamer in the cross-channel and short sea trades. To an ever-increasing extent traffic, be it commercial or holiday makers seeking the sun, demanded the convenience of the anonymous roll on/roll off ferry working a shuttle service between purpose-designed link span terminals, and today these routes, in particular those between Britain, Ireland and the continent are more intensively worked than was ever the case in the past. The bulk of the unaccompanied passenger traffic, including that organised by the 'package tour' industry has, however, been taken over by the international air lines.

Passenger vessels intended primarily for cruising continue to be built in small numbers for operation under the British, Norwegian, Russian and 'convenience' flags, and indeed occasional sailings are offered on the North Atlantic routes, but the day of the passenger 'liner' is ended. Actually this is not quite true, since the withdrawal of the Union Castle service deprived the island of St. Helena, which has no air strip, of its link with the outside world. This gap has now been filled by the St. Helena Shipping Co. who operate the 3150-ton converted cargo ship *St. Helena* (ex *Northland Prince*) between Avonmouth, Las Palmas, Ascension, St. Helena and Capetown. Accommodation is provided for 90 passengers.

Michelangelo 1965 'Italia' Spa di Navigazione. Built, with her sister *Raffaello*, for the 'Italia' Line 'southern' route between Genoa and New York. Photo: E.E.Sigwart

The Passenger Liner – epilogue

For some 120 years passenger liners plied a network of routes linking the maritime states around the world. From the days of the puny side lever engined paddle-steamers to the post-war heyday of the Cunard 'Queens', their rôle remained unchanged in that they provided international communication for the conduct of business, passage for those travelling for personal reasons and an inexpensive berth for migrants.

Today the few remaining ocean passenger vessels, including some purpose-built for the task, are almost exclusively employed in the leisure trade for cruising. Some, such as the 65 863-ton Cunard flagship *Queen Elizabeth II* and the Soviet sisters *Ivan Franco, Aleksandr Pushkin* and *Mikhail Lermontov*, completed between 1964 and 1972, are or have been employed seasonally in the North Atlantic trade, crossing to New York or to Montreal, but these occasional sailings have been able to provide no more than a faint reminder of the past.

Only one passenger steamship survives from the beginning of the period under review, and that is Brunel's *Great Britain*, now being restored in her original building dock in Bristol following an epic salvage operation to rescue her derelict hulk, long since abandoned in the Falkland Islands. However, a number of vessels did give good service for many years, one of the arch survivors being the 322-ton iron screw steamship *Edina* built in 1854 for the Leith, Hull & Hamburgh Steam Packet Co. A barquentine-rigged, clipper-stemmed craft, she was employed in the Hamburg trade for but a few months before being taken up in February 1855 for transport work in connection with the Crimean War. Reboilered in 1861,

the *Edina* was subsequently employed in running the American blockade through to Galveston to load cotton for shipment to Liverpool. Thence she went in 1863 to Australia where eventually she was purchased by Captain William Howard Smith for service in the Queensland coast passenger and general cargo trade. The *Edina* was transferred to Melbourne in 1879 and thereafter worked the 45-mile crossing to Geelong, apart from major refits in 1883 and 1917, until finally she was withdrawn from service and sold in June 1938. Hulked by her new owners she was not finally demolished until 1958.

Another survivor was the Cunard *Parthia*, a 3167-ton iron screw steamer delivered by Wm. Denny & Bros. in December 1870 which worked her owners' New York/Boston services until 1884 when she was taken over by John Elder & Co. in part payment for the *Etruria* and *Umbria*. Subsequently employed in the Pacific service of the Canadian Pacific Railway Co., she was acquired in 1892 by the Northern Pacific Steamship Co. as the *Victoria* and was turned over to a new service, under the British flag, between Tacoma and Hong Kong. Transferred to the US register in 1898, the *Victoria* passed ten years later to the owner-ship of the Alaska Steamship Co. by whom she was employed on the arduous Pacific coast service be-tween Seattle and Skagway in Alaska. Like the *Edina*, the *Victoria* worked on year after year in the coastal trade until finally in August 1952 she was withdrawn from service and laid up at Houghton, Lake Washington. Her end came in 1956 when she was towed away to Osaka for breaking up.

Few vessels achieved, however, the longevity of the

Edina and the *Parthia* whose careers embraced the greater part of the century from the rise of the passenger steamship to the onset of its eventual demise as the travelling public took to the air. The traveller today moves in a vastly different environment to that of the passenger crossing the ocean in a diminutive paddle-steamer lacking any contact with the outside world. Speed is the essence of communication and to the business man time represents money. In the circumstances, surface transport cannot compete and the passenger liner has succumbed as a victim of this speed-conscious age.

Taras Shevchenko 1966 USSR. One of a group of five 20000-ton cruise liners built at Wismar, East Germany, for the Soviet State Shipping company between 1964 and 1972. Photo: E.E.Sigwart

Further reading

Bonsor, Noel *North Atlantic Seaway*. First Edition (1955) and Second Edition, Vol. 1 (1975); Vol. 2 (1978)

Bowen & Macpherson *Mail and Passenger Steamships of the Nineteenth Century* (1928)

Boyd, Cable *A Hundred Years History of the P.&O.* (1937)

Burtt, Frank *Cross Channel and Coastal Passenger Steamers* (1934)

Bushell, T.A. *Royal Mail 1839–1939* (1939)

Duckworth & Langmuir *Clyde and Other Coastal Steamers* (1939 and 1977)

Duckworth & Langmuir *Railway and Other Steamers* (1968)

Fletcher, R.A. *Steamships and Their Story* (1910)

Grasemann & McLachlan *English Channel Packet Boats* (1939)

Gregory, Dixon *Australian Steamships. Past and Present* (1928)

Gropallo, Tomaso *Navi a Vapore ed Armamenti Italiani* (1958)

Holmes, Sir George *Ancient and Modern Ships. Part 2. The Era of Steam, Iron and Steel* (1906)

Kennedy, Captain N. *Records of the Early British Steamships* (1933)

Lytle List *Merchant Steam Vessels of the United States. 1807–68* (1952)

Maber, John M. *North Star to Southern Cross. The Story of the Australasian Seaways* (1967)

Maginnis, A.J. *The North Atlantic Ferry* (1892)

Murray, M. *Ships and South Africa* (1933)

Musk, George *Canadian Pacific Afloat* (1968)

Smith, Captain E.C. *A Short History of Marine Engineering* (1937)

Spratt, H.P. *The Birth of the Steamboat* (1958)

Spratt, H.P. *Marine Engineering* (Science Museum Collection) (1953)

Spratt, H.P. *Transatlantic Paddle Steamers* (1951)

Periodicals

Sea Breezes (Liverpool) (1946–78)

Marine News (Journal of the World Ship Society) (1947–78)